This Address Book belongs to:

My Name	
My Address	
Home	
Work	
Mobile	
E-mail	

A/B

Name	
Address	
Home	Work
Mobile	Birthday
E-mail	
Notes	

Name	
Address	
Home	Work
Mobile	Birthday
E-mail	
Notes	

Name	
Address	
Home	Work
Mobile	Birthday
E-mail	
Notes	

Name	
Address	
Home	Work
Mobile	Birthday
E-mail	
Notes	

A/B

Name	
Address	
Home	Work
Mobile	Birthday
E-mail	
Notes	

Name	
Address	
Home	Work
Mobile	Birthday
E-mail	
Notes	

Name	
Address	
Home	Work
Mobile	Birthday
E-mail	
Notes	

Name	
Address	
Home	Work
Mobile	Birthday
E-mail	
Notes	

A/B

Name	
Address	
Home	Work
Mobile	Birthday
E-mail	
Notes	

Name	
Address	
Home	Work
Mobile	Birthday
E-mail	
Notes	

Name	
Address	
Home	Work
Mobile	Birthday
E-mail	
Notes	

Name	
Address	
Home	Work
Mobile	Birthday
E-mail	
Notes	

A/B

Name	
Address	
Home	Work
Mobile	Birthday
E-mail	
Notes	

Name	
Address	
Home	Work
Mobile	Birthday
E-mail	
Notes	

Name	
Address	
Home	Work
Mobile	Birthday
E-mail	
Notes	

Name	
Address	
Home	Work
Mobile	Birthday
E-mail	
Notes	

A/B

Name	
Address	
Home	Work
Mobile	Birthday
E-mail	
Notes	

Name	
Address	
Home	Work
Mobile	Birthday
E-mail	
Notes	

Name	
Address	
Home	Work
Mobile	Birthday
E-mail	
Notes	

Name	
Address	
Home	Work
Mobile	Birthday
E-mail	
Notes	

A/B

Name	
Address	
Home	Work
Mobile	Birthday
E-mail	
Notes	

Name	
Address	
Home	Work
Mobile	Birthday
E-mail	
Notes	

Name	
Address	
Home	Work
Mobile	Birthday
E-mail	
Notes	

Name	
Address	
Home	Work
Mobile	Birthday
E-mail	
Notes	

A/B

Name	
Address	
Home	Work
Mobile	Birthday
E-mail	
Notes	

Name	
Address	
Home	Work
Mobile	Birthday
E-mail	
Notes	

Name	
Address	
Home	Work
Mobile	Birthday
E-mail	
Notes	

Name	
Address	
Home	Work
Mobile	Birthday
E-mail	
Notes	

C/D

Name	
Address	
Home	Work
Mobile	Birthday
E-mail	
Notes	

Name	
Address	
Home	Work
Mobile	Birthday
E-mail	
Notes	

Name	
Address	
Home	Work
Mobile	Birthday
E-mail	
Notes	

Name	
Address	
Home	Work
Mobile	Birthday
E-mail	
Notes	

C/D

Name	
Address	
Home	Work
Mobile	Birthday
E-mail	
Notes	

Name	
Address	
Home	Work
Mobile	Birthday
E-mail	
Notes	

Name	
Address	
Home	Work
Mobile	Birthday
E-mail	
Notes	

Name	
Address	
Home	Work
Mobile	Birthday
E-mail	
Notes	

C/D

Name	
Address	
Home	Work
Mobile	Birthday
E-mail	
Notes	

Name	
Address	
Home	Work
Mobile	Birthday
E-mail	
Notes	

Name	
Address	
Home	Work
Mobile	Birthday
E-mail	
Notes	

Name	
Address	
Home	Work
Mobile	Birthday
E-mail	
Notes	

C/D

Name	
Address	
Home	Work
Mobile	Birthday
E-mail	
Notes	

Name	
Address	
Home	Work
Mobile	Birthday
E-mail	
Notes	

Name	
Address	
Home	Work
Mobile	Birthday
E-mail	
Notes	

Name	
Address	
Home	Work
Mobile	Birthday
E-mail	
Notes	

C/D

Name	
Address	
Home	Work
Mobile	Birthday
E-mail	
Notes	

Name	
Address	
Home	Work
Mobile	Birthday
E-mail	
Notes	

Name	
Address	
Home	Work
Mobile	Birthday
E-mail	
Notes	

Name	
Address	
Home	Work
Mobile	Birthday
E-mail	
Notes	

C/D

Name	
Address	
Home	Work
Mobile	Birthday
E-mail	
Notes	

Name	
Address	
Home	Work
Mobile	Birthday
E-mail	
Notes	

Name	
Address	
Home	Work
Mobile	Birthday
E-mail	
Notes	

Name	
Address	
Home	Work
Mobile	Birthday
E-mail	
Notes	

C/D

Name	
Address	
Home	Work
Mobile	Birthday
E-mail	
Notes	

Name	
Address	
Home	Work
Mobile	Birthday
E-mail	
Notes	

Name	
Address	
Home	Work
Mobile	Birthday
E-mail	
Notes	

Name	
Address	
Home	Work
Mobile	Birthday
E-mail	
Notes	

E/F

Name	
Address	
Home	Work
Mobile	Birthday
E-mail	
Notes	

Name	
Address	
Home	Work
Mobile	Birthday
E-mail	
Notes	

Name	
Address	
Home	Work
Mobile	Birthday
E-mail	
Notes	

Name	
Address	
Home	Work
Mobile	Birthday
E-mail	
Notes	

E/F

Name	
Address	
Home	Work
Mobile	Birthday
E-mail	
Notes	

Name	
Address	
Home	Work
Mobile	Birthday
E-mail	
Notes	

Name	
Address	
Home	Work
Mobile	Birthday
E-mail	
Notes	

Name	
Address	
Home	Work
Mobile	Birthday
E-mail	
Notes	

E/F

Name	
Address	
Home	Work
Mobile	Birthday
E-mail	
Notes	

Name	
Address	
Home	Work
Mobile	Birthday
E-mail	
Notes	

Name	
Address	
Home	Work
Mobile	Birthday
E-mail	
Notes	

Name	
Address	
Home	Work
Mobile	Birthday
E-mail	
Notes	

E/F

Name	
Address	
Home	Work
Mobile	Birthday
E-mail	
Notes	

Name	
Address	
Home	Work
Mobile	Birthday
E-mail	
Notes	

Name	
Address	
Home	Work
Mobile	Birthday
E-mail	
Notes	

Name	
Address	
Home	Work
Mobile	Birthday
E-mail	
Notes	

E/F

Name	
Address	
Home	Work
Mobile	Birthday
E-mail	
Notes	

Name	
Address	
Home	Work
Mobile	Birthday
E-mail	
Notes	

Name	
Address	
Home	Work
Mobile	Birthday
E-mail	
Notes	

Name	
Address	
Home	Work
Mobile	Birthday
E-mail	
Notes	

E/F

Name	
Address	
Home	Work
Mobile	Birthday
E-mail	
Notes	

Name	
Address	
Home	Work
Mobile	Birthday
E-mail	
Notes	

Name	
Address	
Home	Work
Mobile	Birthday
E-mail	
Notes	

Name	
Address	
Home	Work
Mobile	Birthday
E-mail	
Notes	

E/F

Name	
Address	
Home	Work
Mobile	Birthday
E-mail	
Notes	

Name	
Address	
Home	Work
Mobile	Birthday
E-mail	
Notes	

Name	
Address	
Home	Work
Mobile	Birthday
E-mail	
Notes	

Name	
Address	
Home	Work
Mobile	Birthday
E-mail	
Notes	

G/H

Name	
Address	

Home	Work
Mobile	Birthday

E-mail	
Notes	

Name	
Address	

Home	Work
Mobile	Birthday

E-mail	
Notes	

Name	
Address	

Home	Work
Mobile	Birthday

E-mail	
Notes	

Name	
Address	

Home	Work
Mobile	Birthday

E-mail	
Notes	

G/H

Name	
Address	
Home	Work
Mobile	Birthday
E-mail	
Notes	

Name	
Address	
Home	Work
Mobile	Birthday
E-mail	
Notes	

Name	
Address	
Home	Work
Mobile	Birthday
E-mail	
Notes	

Name	
Address	
Home	Work
Mobile	Birthday
E-mail	
Notes	

G/H

Name	
Address	
Home	Work
Mobile	Birthday
E-mail	
Notes	

Name	
Address	
Home	Work
Mobile	Birthday
E-mail	
Notes	

Name	
Address	
Home	Work
Mobile	Birthday
E-mail	
Notes	

Name	
Address	
Home	Work
Mobile	Birthday
E-mail	
Notes	

G/H

Name	
Address	
Home	Work
Mobile	Birthday
E-mail	
Notes	

Name	
Address	
Home	Work
Mobile	Birthday
E-mail	
Notes	

Name	
Address	
Home	Work
Mobile	Birthday
E-mail	
Notes	

Name	
Address	
Home	Work
Mobile	Birthday
E-mail	
Notes	

G/H

Name	
Address	
Home	Work
Mobile	Birthday
E-mail	
Notes	

Name	
Address	
Home	Work
Mobile	Birthday
E-mail	
Notes	

Name	
Address	
Home	Work
Mobile	Birthday
E-mail	
Notes	

Name	
Address	
Home	Work
Mobile	Birthday
E-mail	
Notes	

G/H

Name	
Address	
Home	Work
Mobile	Birthday
E-mail	
Notes	

Name	
Address	
Home	Work
Mobile	Birthday
E-mail	
Notes	

Name	
Address	
Home	Work
Mobile	Birthday
E-mail	
Notes	

Name	
Address	
Home	Work
Mobile	Birthday
E-mail	
Notes	

G/H

Name	
Address	
Home	Work
Mobile	Birthday
E-mail	
Notes	

Name	
Address	
Home	Work
Mobile	Birthday
E-mail	
Notes	

Name	
Address	
Home	Work
Mobile	Birthday
E-mail	
Notes	

Name	
Address	
Home	Work
Mobile	Birthday
E-mail	
Notes	

I/J

Name	
Address	
Home	Work
Mobile	Birthday
E-mail	
Notes	

Name	
Address	
Home	Work
Mobile	Birthday
E-mail	
Notes	

Name	
Address	
Home	Work
Mobile	Birthday
E-mail	
Notes	

Name	
Address	
Home	Work
Mobile	Birthday
E-mail	
Notes	

I/J

Name	
Address	
Home	Work
Mobile	Birthday
E-mail	
Notes	

Name	
Address	
Home	Work
Mobile	Birthday
E-mail	
Notes	

Name	
Address	
Home	Work
Mobile	Birthday
E-mail	
Notes	

Name	
Address	
Home	Work
Mobile	Birthday
E-mail	
Notes	

I/J

Name	
Address	
Home	Work
Mobile	Birthday
E-mail	
Notes	

Name	
Address	
Home	Work
Mobile	Birthday
E-mail	
Notes	

Name	
Address	
Home	Work
Mobile	Birthday
E-mail	
Notes	

Name	
Address	
Home	Work
Mobile	Birthday
E-mail	
Notes	

I/J

Name	
Address	
Home	Work
Mobile	Birthday
E-mail	
Notes	

Name	
Address	
Home	Work
Mobile	Birthday
E-mail	
Notes	

Name	
Address	
Home	Work
Mobile	Birthday
E-mail	
Notes	

Name	
Address	
Home	Work
Mobile	Birthday
E-mail	
Notes	

I/J

Name	
Address	
Home	Work
Mobile	Birthday
E-mail	
Notes	

Name	
Address	
Home	Work
Mobile	Birthday
E-mail	
Notes	

Name	
Address	
Home	Work
Mobile	Birthday
E-mail	
Notes	

Name	
Address	
Home	Work
Mobile	Birthday
E-mail	
Notes	

I/J

Name	
Address	
Home	Work
Mobile	Birthday
E-mail	
Notes	

Name	
Address	
Home	Work
Mobile	Birthday
E-mail	
Notes	

Name	
Address	
Home	Work
Mobile	Birthday
E-mail	
Notes	

Name	
Address	
Home	Work
Mobile	Birthday
E-mail	
Notes	

I/J

Name	
Address	
Home	Work
Mobile	Birthday
E-mail	
Notes	

Name	
Address	
Home	Work
Mobile	Birthday
E-mail	
Notes	

Name	
Address	
Home	Work
Mobile	Birthday
E-mail	
Notes	

Name	
Address	
Home	Work
Mobile	Birthday
E-mail	
Notes	

K/L

Name	
Address	
Home	Work
Mobile	Birthday
E-mail	
Notes	

Name	
Address	
Home	Work
Mobile	Birthday
E-mail	
Notes	

Name	
Address	
Home	Work
Mobile	Birthday
E-mail	
Notes	

Name	
Address	
Home	Work
Mobile	Birthday
E-mail	
Notes	

K/L

Name	
Address	
Home	Work
Mobile	Birthday
E-mail	
Notes	

Name	
Address	
Home	Work
Mobile	Birthday
E-mail	
Notes	

Name	
Address	
Home	Work
Mobile	Birthday
E-mail	
Notes	

Name	
Address	
Home	Work
Mobile	Birthday
E-mail	
Notes	

K/L

Name	
Address	
Home	Work
Mobile	Birthday
E-mail	
Notes	

Name	
Address	
Home	Work
Mobile	Birthday
E-mail	
Notes	

Name	
Address	
Home	Work
Mobile	Birthday
E-mail	
Notes	

Name	
Address	
Home	Work
Mobile	Birthday
E-mail	
Notes	

K/L

Name	
Address	
Home	Work
Mobile	Birthday
E-mail	
Notes	

Name	
Address	
Home	Work
Mobile	Birthday
E-mail	
Notes	

Name	
Address	
Home	Work
Mobile	Birthday
E-mail	
Notes	

Name	
Address	
Home	Work
Mobile	Birthday
E-mail	
Notes	

K/L

Name	
Address	
Home	Work
Mobile	Birthday
E-mail	
Notes	

Name	
Address	
Home	Work
Mobile	Birthday
E-mail	
Notes	

Name	
Address	
Home	Work
Mobile	Birthday
E-mail	
Notes	

Name	
Address	
Home	Work
Mobile	Birthday
E-mail	
Notes	

K/L

Name	
Address	
Home	Work
Mobile	Birthday
E-mail	
Notes	

Name	
Address	
Home	Work
Mobile	Birthday
E-mail	
Notes	

Name	
Address	
Home	Work
Mobile	Birthday
E-mail	
Notes	

Name	
Address	
Home	Work
Mobile	Birthday
E-mail	
Notes	

K/L

Name	
Address	
Home	Work
Mobile	Birthday
E-mail	
Notes	

Name	
Address	
Home	Work
Mobile	Birthday
E-mail	
Notes	

Name	
Address	
Home	Work
Mobile	Birthday
E-mail	
Notes	

Name	
Address	
Home	Work
Mobile	Birthday
E-mail	
Notes	

M/N

Name	
Address	
Home	Work
Mobile	Birthday
E-mail	
Notes	

Name	
Address	
Home	Work
Mobile	Birthday
E-mail	
Notes	

Name	
Address	
Home	Work
Mobile	Birthday
E-mail	
Notes	

Name	
Address	
Home	Work
Mobile	Birthday
E-mail	
Notes	

M/N

Name	
Address	
Home	Work
Mobile	Birthday
E-mail	
Notes	

Name	
Address	
Home	Work
Mobile	Birthday
E-mail	
Notes	

Name	
Address	
Home	Work
Mobile	Birthday
E-mail	
Notes	

Name	
Address	
Home	Work
Mobile	Birthday
E-mail	
Notes	

M/N

Name	
Address	
Home	Work
Mobile	Birthday
E-mail	
Notes	

Name	
Address	
Home	Work
Mobile	Birthday
E-mail	
Notes	

Name	
Address	
Home	Work
Mobile	Birthday
E-mail	
Notes	

Name	
Address	
Home	Work
Mobile	Birthday
E-mail	
Notes	

M/N

Name	
Address	
Home	Work
Mobile	Birthday
E-mail	
Notes	

Name	
Address	
Home	Work
Mobile	Birthday
E-mail	
Notes	

Name	
Address	
Home	Work
Mobile	Birthday
E-mail	
Notes	

Name	
Address	
Home	Work
Mobile	Birthday
E-mail	
Notes	

M/N

Name	
Address	
Home	Work
Mobile	Birthday
E-mail	
Notes	

Name	
Address	
Home	Work
Mobile	Birthday
E-mail	
Notes	

Name	
Address	
Home	Work
Mobile	Birthday
E-mail	
Notes	

Name	
Address	
Home	Work
Mobile	Birthday
E-mail	
Notes	

M/N

Name	
Address	
Home	Work
Mobile	Birthday
E-mail	
Notes	

Name	
Address	
Home	Work
Mobile	Birthday
E-mail	
Notes	

Name	
Address	
Home	Work
Mobile	Birthday
E-mail	
Notes	

Name	
Address	
Home	Work
Mobile	Birthday
E-mail	
Notes	

M/N

Name	
Address	
Home	Work
Mobile	Birthday
E-mail	
Notes	

Name	
Address	
Home	Work
Mobile	Birthday
E-mail	
Notes	

Name	
Address	
Home	Work
Mobile	Birthday
E-mail	
Notes	

Name	
Address	
Home	Work
Mobile	Birthday
E-mail	
Notes	

O/P

Name	
Address	
Home	Work
Mobile	Birthday
E-mail	
Notes	

Name	
Address	
Home	Work
Mobile	Birthday
E-mail	
Notes	

Name	
Address	
Home	Work
Mobile	Birthday
E-mail	
Notes	

Name	
Address	
Home	Work
Mobile	Birthday
E-mail	
Notes	

O/P

Name	
Address	
Home	Work
Mobile	Birthday
E-mail	
Notes	

Name	
Address	
Home	Work
Mobile	Birthday
E-mail	
Notes	

Name	
Address	
Home	Work
Mobile	Birthday
E-mail	
Notes	

Name	
Address	
Home	Work
Mobile	Birthday
E-mail	
Notes	

O/P

Name	
Address	
Home	Work
Mobile	Birthday
E-mail	
Notes	

Name	
Address	
Home	Work
Mobile	Birthday
E-mail	
Notes	

Name	
Address	
Home	Work
Mobile	Birthday
E-mail	
Notes	

Name	
Address	
Home	Work
Mobile	Birthday
E-mail	
Notes	

O/P

Name	
Address	
Home	Work
Mobile	Birthday
E-mail	
Notes	

Name	
Address	
Home	Work
Mobile	Birthday
E-mail	
Notes	

Name	
Address	
Home	Work
Mobile	Birthday
E-mail	
Notes	

Name	
Address	
Home	Work
Mobile	Birthday
E-mail	
Notes	

O/P

Name	
Address	
Home	Work
Mobile	Birthday
E-mail	
Notes	

Name	
Address	
Home	Work
Mobile	Birthday
E-mail	
Notes	

Name	
Address	
Home	Work
Mobile	Birthday
E-mail	
Notes	

Name	
Address	
Home	Work
Mobile	Birthday
E-mail	
Notes	

O/P

Name	
Address	
Home	Work
Mobile	Birthday
E-mail	
Notes	

Name	
Address	
Home	Work
Mobile	Birthday
E-mail	
Notes	

Name	
Address	
Home	Work
Mobile	Birthday
E-mail	
Notes	

Name	
Address	
Home	Work
Mobile	Birthday
E-mail	
Notes	

O/P

Name	
Address	
Home	Work
Mobile	Birthday
E-mail	
Notes	

Name	
Address	
Home	Work
Mobile	Birthday
E-mail	
Notes	

Name	
Address	
Home	Work
Mobile	Birthday
E-mail	
Notes	

Name	
Address	
Home	Work
Mobile	Birthday
E-mail	
Notes	

Q/R

Name	
Address	
Home	Work
Mobile	Birthday
E-mail	
Notes	

Name	
Address	
Home	Work
Mobile	Birthday
E-mail	
Notes	

Name	
Address	
Home	Work
Mobile	Birthday
E-mail	
Notes	

Name	
Address	
Home	Work
Mobile	Birthday
E-mail	
Notes	

Q/R

Name	
Address	
Home	Work
Mobile	Birthday
E-mail	
Notes	

Name	
Address	
Home	Work
Mobile	Birthday
E-mail	
Notes	

Name	
Address	
Home	Work
Mobile	Birthday
E-mail	
Notes	

Name	
Address	
Home	Work
Mobile	Birthday
E-mail	
Notes	

Q/R

Name	Elisabeth Rose
Address	1 Wuy close West busbyt Surrey nt 46rs

Home		Work	
Mobile		Birthday	1st Agest
E-mail			
Notes			

Name	
Address	

Home		Work	
Mobile		Birthday	
E-mail			
Notes			

Name	
Address	

Home		Work	
Mobile		Birthday	
E-mail			
Notes			

Name	
Address	

Home		Work	
Mobile		Birthday	
E-mail			
Notes			

Q/R

Name	
Address	
Home	Work
Mobile	Birthday
E-mail	
Notes	

Name	
Address	
Home	Work
Mobile	Birthday
E-mail	
Notes	

Name	
Address	
Home	Work
Mobile	Birthday
E-mail	
Notes	

Name	
Address	
Home	Work
Mobile	Birthday
E-mail	
Notes	

Q/R

Name	
Address	
Home	Work
Mobile	Birthday
E-mail	
Notes	

Name	
Address	
Home	Work
Mobile	Birthday
E-mail	
Notes	

Name	
Address	
Home	Work
Mobile	Birthday
E-mail	
Notes	

Name	
Address	
Home	Work
Mobile	Birthday
E-mail	
Notes	

Q/R

Name	
Address	
Home	Work
Mobile	Birthday
E-mail	
Notes	

Name	
Address	
Home	Work
Mobile	Birthday
E-mail	
Notes	

Name	
Address	
Home	Work
Mobile	Birthday
E-mail	
Notes	

Name	
Address	
Home	Work
Mobile	Birthday
E-mail	
Notes	

Q/R

Name	
Address	
Home	Work
Mobile	Birthday
E-mail	
Notes	

Name	
Address	
Home	Work
Mobile	Birthday
E-mail	
Notes	

Name	
Address	
Home	Work
Mobile	Birthday
E-mail	
Notes	

Name	
Address	
Home	Work
Mobile	Birthday
E-mail	
Notes	

S/T

Name	
Address	
Home	Work
Mobile	Birthday
E-mail	
Notes	

Name	
Address	
Home	Work
Mobile	Birthday
E-mail	
Notes	

Name	
Address	
Home	Work
Mobile	Birthday
E-mail	
Notes	

Name	
Address	
Home	Work
Mobile	Birthday
E-mail	
Notes	

S/T

Name	
Address	
Home	Work
Mobile	Birthday
E-mail	
Notes	

Name	
Address	
Home	Work
Mobile	Birthday
E-mail	
Notes	

Name	
Address	
Home	Work
Mobile	Birthday
E-mail	
Notes	

Name	
Address	
Home	Work
Mobile	Birthday
E-mail	
Notes	

S/T

Name	
Address	
Home	Work
Mobile	Birthday
E-mail	
Notes	

Name	
Address	
Home	Work
Mobile	Birthday
E-mail	
Notes	

Name	
Address	
Home	Work
Mobile	Birthday
E-mail	
Notes	

Name	
Address	
Home	Work
Mobile	Birthday
E-mail	
Notes	

S/T

Name	
Address	
Home	Work
Mobile	Birthday
E-mail	
Notes	

Name	
Address	
Home	Work
Mobile	Birthday
E-mail	
Notes	

Name	
Address	
Home	Work
Mobile	Birthday
E-mail	
Notes	

Name	
Address	
Home	Work
Mobile	Birthday
E-mail	
Notes	

S/T

Name	
Address	
Home	Work
Mobile	Birthday
E-mail	
Notes	

Name	
Address	
Home	Work
Mobile	Birthday
E-mail	
Notes	

Name	
Address	
Home	Work
Mobile	Birthday
E-mail	
Notes	

Name	
Address	
Home	Work
Mobile	Birthday
E-mail	
Notes	

S/T

Name	
Address	
Home	Work
Mobile	Birthday
E-mail	
Notes	

Name	
Address	
Home	Work
Mobile	Birthday
E-mail	
Notes	

Name	
Address	
Home	Work
Mobile	Birthday
E-mail	
Notes	

Name	
Address	
Home	Work
Mobile	Birthday
E-mail	
Notes	

S/T

Name	
Address	
Home	Work
Mobile	Birthday
E-mail	
Notes	

Name	
Address	
Home	Work
Mobile	Birthday
E-mail	
Notes	

Name	
Address	
Home	Work
Mobile	Birthday
E-mail	
Notes	

Name	
Address	
Home	Work
Mobile	Birthday
E-mail	
Notes	

U/V

Name	
Address	
Home	Work
Mobile	Birthday
E-mail	
Notes	

Name	
Address	
Home	Work
Mobile	Birthday
E-mail	
Notes	

Name	
Address	
Home	Work
Mobile	Birthday
E-mail	
Notes	

Name	
Address	
Home	Work
Mobile	Birthday
E-mail	
Notes	

U/V

Name	
Address	
Home	Work
Mobile	Birthday
E-mail	
Notes	

Name	
Address	
Home	Work
Mobile	Birthday
E-mail	
Notes	

Name	
Address	
Home	Work
Mobile	Birthday
E-mail	
Notes	

Name	
Address	
Home	Work
Mobile	Birthday
E-mail	
Notes	

U/V

Name	
Address	
Home	Work
Mobile	Birthday
E-mail	
Notes	

Name	
Address	
Home	Work
Mobile	Birthday
E-mail	
Notes	

Name	
Address	
Home	Work
Mobile	Birthday
E-mail	
Notes	

Name	
Address	
Home	Work
Mobile	Birthday
E-mail	
Notes	

U/V

Name	
Address	
Home	Work
Mobile	Birthday
E-mail	
Notes	

Name	
Address	
Home	Work
Mobile	Birthday
E-mail	
Notes	

Name	
Address	
Home	Work
Mobile	Birthday
E-mail	
Notes	

Name	
Address	
Home	Work
Mobile	Birthday
E-mail	
Notes	

U/V

Name	
Address	
Home	Work
Mobile	Birthday
E-mail	
Notes	

Name	
Address	
Home	Work
Mobile	Birthday
E-mail	
Notes	

Name	
Address	
Home	Work
Mobile	Birthday
E-mail	
Notes	

Name	
Address	
Home	Work
Mobile	Birthday
E-mail	
Notes	

U/V

Name	
Address	
Home	Work
Mobile	Birthday
E-mail	
Notes	

Name	
Address	
Home	Work
Mobile	Birthday
E-mail	
Notes	

Name	
Address	
Home	Work
Mobile	Birthday
E-mail	
Notes	

Name	
Address	
Home	Work
Mobile	Birthday
E-mail	
Notes	

U/V

Name	
Address	
Home	Work
Mobile	Birthday
E-mail	
Notes	

Name	
Address	
Home	Work
Mobile	Birthday
E-mail	
Notes	

Name	
Address	
Home	Work
Mobile	Birthday
E-mail	
Notes	

Name	
Address	
Home	Work
Mobile	Birthday
E-mail	
Notes	

W/X

Name	
Address	
Home	Work
Mobile	Birthday
E-mail	
Notes	

Name	
Address	
Home	Work
Mobile	Birthday
E-mail	
Notes	

Name	
Address	
Home	Work
Mobile	Birthday
E-mail	
Notes	

Name	
Address	
Home	Work
Mobile	Birthday
E-mail	
Notes	

W/X

Name	
Address	
Home	Work
Mobile	Birthday
E-mail	
Notes	

Name	
Address	
Home	Work
Mobile	Birthday
E-mail	
Notes	

Name	
Address	
Home	Work
Mobile	Birthday
E-mail	
Notes	

Name	
Address	
Home	Work
Mobile	Birthday
E-mail	
Notes	

W/X

Name	
Address	
Home	Work
Mobile	Birthday
E-mail	
Notes	

Name	
Address	
Home	Work
Mobile	Birthday
E-mail	
Notes	

Name	
Address	
Home	Work
Mobile	Birthday
E-mail	
Notes	

Name	
Address	
Home	Work
Mobile	Birthday
E-mail	
Notes	

W/X

Name	
Address	
Home	Work
Mobile	Birthday
E-mail	
Notes	

Name	
Address	
Home	Work
Mobile	Birthday
E-mail	
Notes	

Name	
Address	
Home	Work
Mobile	Birthday
E-mail	
Notes	

Name	
Address	
Home	Work
Mobile	Birthday
E-mail	
Notes	

W/X

Name	
Address	
Home	Work
Mobile	Birthday
E-mail	
Notes	

Name	
Address	
Home	Work
Mobile	Birthday
E-mail	
Notes	

Name	
Address	
Home	Work
Mobile	Birthday
E-mail	
Notes	

Name	
Address	
Home	Work
Mobile	Birthday
E-mail	
Notes	

W/X

Name	
Address	
Home	Work
Mobile	Birthday
E-mail	
Notes	

Name	
Address	
Home	Work
Mobile	Birthday
E-mail	
Notes	

Name	
Address	
Home	Work
Mobile	Birthday
E-mail	
Notes	

Name	
Address	
Home	Work
Mobile	Birthday
E-mail	
Notes	

W/X

Name	
Address	
Home	Work
Mobile	Birthday
E-mail	
Notes	

Name	
Address	
Home	Work
Mobile	Birthday
E-mail	
Notes	

Name	
Address	
Home	Work
Mobile	Birthday
E-mail	
Notes	

Name	
Address	
Home	Work
Mobile	Birthday
E-mail	
Notes	

Y/Z

Name	
Address	
Home	Work
Mobile	Birthday
E-mail	
Notes	

Name	
Address	
Home	Work
Mobile	Birthday
E-mail	
Notes	

Name	
Address	
Home	Work
Mobile	Birthday
E-mail	
Notes	

Name	
Address	
Home	Work
Mobile	Birthday
E-mail	
Notes	

Y/Z

Name	
Address	
Home	Work
Mobile	Birthday
E-mail	
Notes	

Name	
Address	
Home	Work
Mobile	Birthday
E-mail	
Notes	

Name	
Address	
Home	Work
Mobile	Birthday
E-mail	
Notes	

Name	
Address	
Home	Work
Mobile	Birthday
E-mail	
Notes	

Y/Z

Name	
Address	
Home	Work
Mobile	Birthday
E-mail	
Notes	

Name	
Address	
Home	Work
Mobile	Birthday
E-mail	
Notes	

Name	
Address	
Home	Work
Mobile	Birthday
E-mail	
Notes	

Name	
Address	
Home	Work
Mobile	Birthday
E-mail	
Notes	

Y/Z

Name	
Address	
Home	Work
Mobile	Birthday
E-mail	
Notes	

Name	
Address	
Home	Work
Mobile	Birthday
E-mail	
Notes	

Name	
Address	
Home	Work
Mobile	Birthday
E-mail	
Notes	

Name	
Address	
Home	Work
Mobile	Birthday
E-mail	
Notes	

Y/Z

Name	
Address	
Home	Work
Mobile	Birthday
E-mail	
Notes	

Name	
Address	
Home	Work
Mobile	Birthday
E-mail	
Notes	

Name	
Address	
Home	Work
Mobile	Birthday
E-mail	
Notes	

Name	
Address	
Home	Work
Mobile	Birthday
E-mail	
Notes	

Y/Z

Name	
Address	
Home	Work
Mobile	Birthday
E-mail	
Notes	

Name	
Address	
Home	Work
Mobile	Birthday
E-mail	
Notes	

Name	
Address	
Home	Work
Mobile	Birthday
E-mail	
Notes	

Name	
Address	
Home	Work
Mobile	Birthday
E-mail	
Notes	

Y/Z

Name	
Address	
Home	Work
Mobile	Birthday
E-mail	
Notes	

Name	
Address	
Home	Work
Mobile	Birthday
E-mail	
Notes	

Name	
Address	
Home	Work
Mobile	Birthday
E-mail	
Notes	

Name	
Address	
Home	Work
Mobile	Birthday
E-mail	
Notes	

Printed in Great Britain
by Amazon

16602032R00058